Poetry

(IS) ME

KEVIN E. BROWN

outskirts
press

Outskirts Press, Inc.
http://www.outskirtspress.com

ISBN: 978-1-9772-2336-4

Outskirts Press and the "OP" logo are trademarks belonging to Outskirts Press, Inc.

PRINTED IN THE UNITED STATES OF AMERICA

Welcome to my mind,
a creation of art, from
over the years...

About the Author

Kevin is a graduate from Virginia Commonwealth University and currently resides outside of Washington, D.C.

In the early 2000's, he took up writing as an interest back in High School when his class was tasked with a project to create a Poetry book from scratch. His Father, Ronald Brown, with experience in graphic design helped him put together an amazing, colorful, and fully laminated collection of stories, all written by Kevin himself.

That's when he realized that his creative thinking began to flourish.

Ideas, words, and phrases started to appear before his mind. A vision was born, and it was at that moment that he knew that making a difference was something he wanted to achieve. By sharing his thoughts with the world, no matter how random they might be on paper, Kevin leads by example by encouraging his readers to seek out, chase down, capture, and claim the life that they deserve.

Continuing to write in his free time, it wasn't until 2009 when his collection of work started to grow exponentially. In 2011, his poem *Opposite World* won first place in the *D.C. Spotlight Newspaper* Poetry contest. He was interviewed and featured in their online paper which is still available today to read. Despite entering several other contests, this was the only contest Kevin had won with the exception of a few honorable mentions. However, he was not discouraged, and he never gave up on his goals and dreams as a writer; no matter how long it took to manifest into his reality.

After the passing of his Father back in July of 2018, Kevin's thoughts and emotions really started to emerge. Losing his Father led him to discover more about life and who he truly was after experiencing what is called a Spiritual Awakening. He had no idea why he was feeling the way he was feeling, and why a lot of the things he enjoyed, he no longer cared for. Nevertheless, his passion for writing and helping people grow and move past their traumas and pains motivated him in a monumental way.

Kevin wanted to share his story with the world and help people move optimistically through theirs. Since his Father's passing, Kevin took interest in obtaining a Life Coach Certification because he holds a passion for helping people and putting a smile on someone's face, which he always was able to do. He also took his Life Coaching and enthusiasm for positivity to another level by creating a YouTube channel and brand, called *Speak it, See it, Feel it*.

Now, as a Certified Law of Attraction Life Coach and YouTube vlogger, Kevin produces positive messages weekly on his channel by helping people push through life and understand more of who they are. If you are in need of some inspiration or a pick me up throughout your day, this book *Poetry is Me*, along with his channel *Speak it, See it, Feel it* will deliver exactly what you need. It will help you maintain positive energy, and get you moving in the right direction for a happier and more enjoyable life.

Subscribe/follow Kevin's channel by searching for his pen name: **ExpressedWordz** on YouTube.

You are blessed beyond measures and great things are coming your way!

Dedication Page

In Loving Memory of Ronald E. Brown

11/30/57 ~ 7/14/18

To my Father, the greatest man I've ever known, thank you for your guidance and for showing me what it means to be a Father, and how to be loved by one. You have equipped me with everything I need along this journey to sustain the wiles of this world. Your love and care for my Mother, Kathy Brown, is a representation of how love should be spread amongst us all, and you portrayed that every single day.

Dad, because of who you are you have received your wings, and your soul walks freely through the Heavens. As new chapters for me start to begin, watching your strength and perseverance through life is helping me push through the most difficult time of mine, missing and needing you...

'As I sit outside and watch the night clouds move swiftly in my view, I can see that you are there, I know it is you. I can't believe you are gone, but why, is it true? Please God give me the strength, to endure this pain that bleeds through. No matter what happens now, I'm your boy, I will pull through. I'm a Brown, you gave me that name, so I'll see it all the way through. I feel weak when I'm strong, what do I do, I still need you. But I know that I'm your boy, and I'll conquer life, because I'm you...'

Contents

A Passion for Writing 1

Words on Fire 2

Missing You 3

Reaching for the Stars 4

Eyes of an Unborn Soul 5

His Thoughts of Her – (Part 1) 6

Always Stay Positive 7

Whispers from the Wind 8

The Art of a Lady 10

The Angels Will Dance 11

I Am a Disguise 12

Her Thoughts of Him – (Part 2) 13

An Opposite World 14

Stars Wrapped in Skin 15

Faded Time 16

Inspiring Voices 17

Trapped in Sorrow 18

The Regrets of Yesterday 20

Like Father, Like Son 21

Words Coated in Gold 22

The Circle of Life 23

Failure on Earth 24

Falling Skies 25

A Reunited Thought – (Part 3 Final) 26

From Rags to Riches 28

Where Beauty is Found 29

The New World 30

Paint Your Perfect Scene 31

My Guardian Angel 32

His Road to Salvation 33

I Can Hear your Pain 34

An Unknown Era 35

A Child's Birdie 36

I Can, and I Will 37

The Angel by Your Side 38

A Loving World 40

Her Dark Twisted Paradise 41

You are More 43

Spending the Day with Jesus 44

The Love of a Mother 46

The Day I Touched the Clouds 47

The Most Fascinating, Person I Never Met 48

Life After Death 50

The Awakening 52

Poetry is Me 54

Conclusion 55

A Passion for Writing

When pen meets pad and glides across the page

Everything around me becomes silent and staged

I sit back, and start to think real hard

As these thoughts become reality, they come straight from the heart

When did this happen, to feel this great passion

All I can think about is new titles and captions

This God given talent is filled with excitement

When I recite thoughts in my mind, I need something to
    write with

I sit back and smile, after reading these poems

Because I know one day, a lot of people will know them

God has blessed me, He's at work, its' exciting

And I have developed "A Passion for Writing"

Message from the Author:

The collections you are reading are works that I randomly wrote over the years in a ripped-up notepad that I carried around with me. Sit back and enjoy, and welcome to my colorful journey of a mind...

Words on Fire

Who thought of the word, "word?" Where did it originate
   from?

Small letters put together that's pronounced from our tongue

Think hard, about what words will state

And how our brain can process the meaning they make

Words are strong, they can be bad or be good

Show love or show hate, and express each mood

It's amazing, that we can say what we think

Pulling words from our thoughts to mold and shape

It's a three-thought process – think, speak, write

And just like my work, I think then recite

Twisting up words in the core of my brain

To straighten them out and speculate what I'm saying

I can say one thing, but it could mean something different

Can you distinguish the two, from one word to a sentence?

I can start to speak, visualize and then crop it

Just give me a title and I'll free write on that topic

With my pad I'm at peace, with my pen I'm inspired

When giving birth to new thoughts, I create "Words on Fire"

Missing You

I grew up around you, from a boy to a man

You were the center of our family, we revolved around your plan

If we did something wrong and didn't know why

We could always turn to you as our go to guy

You were smarter than ever, heart soft as a feather

You always protected us when encountered by bad weather

You showed us the way, and taught us new things

Our mind and our body will always rest on your wings

The day you left earth, I saw rays in the sky

As you smiled down upon us, saying "My family don't cry"

I reached out my hand because your presence was near

Hearing whispers of your voice, saying "Grandson I'm here"

The passion of this poem is so emotionally anointing

As I feel your presence hold me, my pen begins glowing

As I continue to write, producing tears I need tissues

Please watch over us, because we love and really miss you...

Reaching for the Stars

With an endless imagination, all your dreams can come true

Heart and determination is the number one clue

Don't think small, think big as a star

And never give up when times get hard

Back to the clue, do you know what you want?

If the passion's in your heart, you're now determined to start

But don't get discouraged, people will want you to fail

That should be encouragement for you to prevail

Now clue two, do whatever it takes

And keep your eyes on the prize, there will be mistakes

But you did it, you're there, how did you make it this far

Just smile and tell people that you "Reached for the Stars"

Message from the Author:

My words are filled with encouragement, love, peace, and your wildest imagination. After all, you are a Spiritual Being. If you can see it, then believe you can achieve it. Nothing is too impossible for you to accomplish. Go after what you want, your attitude and dedication is a key element to your success.

Eyes of an Unborn Soul

He looks into our world from a place we can't see

Like Diamonds, Rubies, and Pearls; scattered across our floor seas

How can he see this place, if he physically just doesn't exist?

Created by the God's causes that vision to have some bliss

Do you see it? Look closer, and your eyes will visualize

The pupils in his eyes is some color I cannot describe

Locked behind a realm, a two-sided piece of glass

When looked upon we see our self, but he sees future and past

Crying beneath the rain, causes the oceans to have some rage

When trapped inside a cage, it's like our life has skipped a page

You will see him in your sleep, because he paints the perfect dream

A steady hand he calls art, creates immortal scenes

Think about the things, you try and reach, but cause strain

He sees a calling on your name, so don't you dare feel ashamed

Rain in this timeframe are really tears' from fallen souls

He hides them with the clouds, poured down on a world so cold

My thoughts are getting deeper, can you feel the story I told?

Living in this life span has shown the...

"Eyes of an Unborn Soul"

His Thoughts of Her ~ (Part 1)

This lonely man's vision has been stuck at sea
Everything he sees brings thoughts of she
When he reads, he hears her voice, even eats her favorite foods
Other women want a chance, but to him it would be rude
He stares at frustration, would give the world to bring her back
He's stuck in this woman's world, and moving on is what he lacks
Even the smallest things, like the laundry full of lint
Leaves him smelling clothes, inhaling up her scent
Picturing her lying down is just a beauty to his eyes
Making love was even better, but playing the role his mind denies
Placing his face in his palms and filling them up with tears
Because this man can't seem to control, the life this girl steers
When he sleeps it's only worse, because he only dreams of she
Waking up sometimes mad because it showed how close they'd be
Every woman he'll pass, resemble her so he'll stare
From the sound of heels clicking, to the dresses that they wear
This man can't seem to quit, from what they had and what
   they were
So, he's left with one decision, to continue…
"His Thoughts of Her"

Always Stay Positive

Negativity awakes, when life deals different cards
But if you train your mind right, it'll be done before it starts
I know life is hard, with so much weight on your shoulders
But with one positive thought, you will start to move forward
Don't look back, at all the things that went wrong
Strive to be better, and continue to stand strong
Pray every day and thank God for what you have
Acknowledge His name and He'll reveal more paths
Smile every day, your alive! You can breathe!
The finer things in life is where your mindset should be
Expand your mind higher, and visualize those brighter days
Don't talk down upon yourself, you should give yourself praise
I know one thing, if you live like this
Negativity can't awake, because your mind will resist
Don't look upset and have positive thought blocking
Be happy and excited, you never know whose watching
You know how different keys, will open certain doors
Well the key to positivity, can open up the world
Be sharp and stay focused, be that positive human being
Life is too short to get mad at little things
If you trust my words, be happy and cognitive
Your entire life will change and you'll "Always Stay Positive"

Whispers from the Wind

On a dark cold night, I catch a chill from a silent breeze

The flashlight in the sky creates shadows on fallen trees

I can see my breath, fingers cold in this place

My tongue is now numb, therefore, I have no taste

Listen, do you hear? That soft voice outside my ears?

I close my eyes to focus in, but the sounds have disappeared

Could it be my inner voice, telling me which way to go?

Or is it pushing me towards, a place I do not know?

Hush!! There is it, I hear that voice again

The sound is headed right, and the thrill is seeking in

The hairs on my arms stand, now the path is getting dark

I hear howls and moans, and the occasional growls and barks

I don't know what to do, I'm walking blind it's unsafe

The voice says have Faith, looks deceive to break our Faith

Try to listen closer, let it drift you somewhere new

If you're not happy where you are, make some tweaks and
    tighten screws

Sometimes you have to trust, those things you cannot see

You'll never know the outcome, or how great your life can be

March to your own band, this world was meant to harm and
    bend

Sometimes you will walk in the dark, so listen to…

"Whispers from the Wind"

The Art of a Lady

The beauty in my eyes, reflects what I see

When they walk pass and smile, there's a trembling in the knees

Their voice is so calming, it can heal, it can soothe

Their instinct to protect will turn an enemy into food

From their hair to their eyes, amazing legs and flawless thighs

Will leave a man thinking, "Now that's an Angel in disguise!"

They love, they share, they rejoice, they care

They ask about your day and calm nerves when you are scared

There's something about their walk, when they click from heel
     to heel

They have that special stride because your vision they seem to steal

Hold a rose to her face and make a frame with your thumbs

Squint your eye and take a picture of two beauties under the sun

When a woman's fed up, saying whatever and just stares

Better make it right because in her mind she still cares

They show lots of emotion, they can have lots of rage

But a woman likes to talk, it's their nature to engage

Show respect to Earth's queens, don't be rude and act crazy

One of the finest things in life is…

"The Art Of A Lady"

The Angels Will Dance

November 22nd, the Lord called your name

Darkness filled our hearts, but no longer you're in pain

A part of you lies, within the tears on our face

As those tears hit our hands, that part of you we take

A woman of pure strength, she stood so strong

Was our guidance in the dark, when days seemed to be wrong

A Queen of our King, Thomas E. Brown

Reunited once again with a Welcome Home crown

Protect over our family, shield us with your wings

We promise to stick together, for what these years bring

Even though my heart aches, I'm happy that you're free

Sitting on your throne, looking down on top of me

I will miss you very much, and cherish the moments shared

Time heals wounds, and broken hearts are repaired

So now that your home, filled with joy and romance

Sing along with the Lord, and…

"The Angels Will Dance"

I Am a Disguise

I am who I am, for the reason I've been placed

Intertwining the word "help," gives that reason here some taste

Your life is like some clay, I can mold, I can shape

Why let your heart break, to be stomped and replaced?

From "Words on Fire" to "Always Staying Positive"

My words here are real, it's the reason why I live

My paper is my Father, my Mother is my pen

A vision above the clouds, causes my ink to have no end

Motivation's my middle name, determination I shall claim

To drive prosperity lane, is a first class Universal plane

I am an ocean that roars, underneath the bright moon

Drifting in the wind, consumed by monsoons

I am who I am, do you see the inner me?

A heart made of gold, eternal life created me

My presence is in the air, soaring high just like the birds

Something precious like my words, creates an audience like
    cattle herds

I am who I am, I've planted seeds across this land

The "Trapped in Sorrow" man, needs my hand to help him stand

Can you see it now, just look closely with your eyes

I am who I am, because I'm different, that's my disguise…

Her Thoughts of Him ~ (Part 2)

A soft heart she has, in the process of being healed

His cologne drifts by, with the wind while in the fields

A pondering mind she has, "Well does he ever think of me?"

But little does she know, in his dreams, she's all he sees

Many guys have asked her out, but she's just not in the mood

"Is he seeing other woman, or does he think that it is rude?"

One week a month, brings emotional and lots of rage

She's crying and needs affection, but afraid to engage

She writes in her journal, about the times they had

But tears hit the page, smearing her words because she's sad

There's no doubt she's at a loss, and her life is off track

She wants to feel complete, but missing a piece is what she lacks

It's hard for her to sleep, when she just tosses and turns

She could write a book titled, "When a Female's Concerned"

This woman can't seem to quit, from traveling a life that
  seems dim

So, she's left with one decision, to continue…

"Her Thoughts of Him"

An Opposite World

What would it be like to switch our right and left shoe?

What if the sky was green and the grass was blue?

What if the Universe was Earth and our world was called Space?

Does that mean aliens live here with no trace of human race?

How about if we read from the right to the left?

And the meaning of blind was defined as deaf

If our world was like this, would we be confused and ask how?

Writing this same exact poem, but mind painting our world now

What if everything was perfect, no disasters and no crime?

And when you made a mistake, you could turn back time?

What if music was called games and what you heard was called
   playing?

Fire was ice cold, and ice was hot blazing

What if the number two really meant zero, none?

And the end of a story was where it really begun

Would everyone be scared to live in this world for a day?

Probably, besides we've only seen one way

What if a King was called Queen and a Queen was called King?

And when you were full really meant you were starving

Planes don't fly here, here they sail and ship

Its' like going back in time and seeing the world has flipped

Now that I altered your perception and got your mind all curled

You just took a look at "An Opposite World"

Stars Wrapped in Skin

I don't think I'm from here, this planet we live seems mighty
strange

There are realms we cannot see, humanity is broken and needs
to change

Something is holding us back, from discovering our true being

The Universe holds the answer, and within us lies the true
meaning

From the start of our creation, to the grounds we stand now

Our souls say to love, but our human just won't allow

Vibrations and frequencies are the energies we need

If we destroy every seed, then the rain can't sprout our deeds

We all have these emotions, that's connected to steer our life

If you live with love and light, these negative emotions cannot
fight

So, rise up and stand tall, be that soul that's deep within

We are magic and Spiritual beings, we are cosmic "Stars
Wrapped in Skin"

Faded Time

Awaiting the cloak of day, with many sleepless nights
Fog thick like smoke, leaves his vision trying to fight
Staring at the clock, when one minutes seems like five
Pacing back and forth, his thought process is denied
Weary from trying to think, about his life and where he stands
A cold dinner plate, attracts the flies and not this man
He keeps the lights dim and lets the breeze in the room
Bored and confused counting bristles on a broom
Five minutes pass, equals one minute that's gone by
He sits to huff and puff, the occasional roll of eyes
He's stuck in a child's body, and playing games runs his mind
The clock ticks backwards, reversing the hands of time
Is he stuck in a realm, where each minute seems long?
Because his state of self-consciousness says something's wrong
If he's trapped in a child's body as those hands reverse back
The cure to being young has created its' first match
The wrinkles on his hands, they disappear, so now they're smooth
His smile is coming back, regaining a child's playful mood
He jumps up and down, he finally can, and he should
He looks back on his life, because he had no childhood
His alarm goes off, it's time for school it's almost nine
Waking up from a dream gave him a taste of "Faded Time"

Inspiring Voices

A troubled teen has fallen down, headed left instead of right
Not a soul to pick him up, he doesn't listen, only fights
We cannot blame this child for the path he is trying to chase
Because the environment he is in, breaks down the human race
Role models can't be found, positivity doesn't exist
To wake up in the morning is not a blessing, but a wish
Powders from guns fill the air, startling animals and the birds
Watch me change his life, with the power behind my words
I told him on that path, the road to misbehave
Will lead him in two directions, in a cell or in a grave
Positivity brings success, a different life he cannot see
At least join the Army, and be all that you can be
Your family disappeared, it's your fault to have pushed them away
The blessing behind my words will never leave, but forever stay
I'm trying to grasp the life, of someone with inner pain
His attitude refrains, but there's a calling on my name
Buying drugs and following thugs
His life's plan equals shoulder shrugs
I told him I will try, to help give him a fresh start
Using the power of spoken art to create goodness in thy heart
Create your own destiny and make the right choices
By living a better life and following…
"Inspiring Voices"

Trapped in Sorrow

I must save this man, from the pain he feels

Caught by darkness, no emotions reveal

Saddened by the wind that sways across his face

His eyes seem to burn, mind painting the disgrace

No shoulder to lean on, nobody to call

His hearts at the bottom, of a pit he didn't fall

Searching up and down, for a way to replace

That hole in his chest, which contains air and space

That frown on his face, is fake with no shape

Even his favorite foods, leave him eating with no taste

His stomach starts to turn, his head begins to ache

Water drips from his eyes, because his thoughts won the race

I should get down on my knee, and lend him a hand

Picking up the man, from the tears he stands

As I try to reach out, my hand he takes

But his skin is so cold, my body starts to shake

He looked up, with crystal blue tears

Saying, "There's no point, because I've been here for years"

He said his heart hurts, it's in a pit he can't find

And time after time left him emotionally blind

I said, "I can help, I'll find a rope that I can borrow"

But he said, "There's no point."

Because he's "Trapped in Sorrow"

Message from the Author:

Every day, people are battling with certain things in their life that has taken a toll on them and possibly everyone around them. Depression, anxiety, suicide, grief, addiction... the list goes on. However, you never know who that soul could be that's going through that battle. Some people show it without a care while others have the tendency to hide it very well in plain sight. No matter what your situation is, be that dope, loving and kind soul to everyone you come across. Your positive energy will come back to you in unexpected ways.

The Regrets of Yesterday

This woman lies in his bed, but he smiles like nothing's wrong

But in his heart, he must confess, in this place he doesn't belong

He hides his weary face which contains silent tears

She sneaks behind to kiss his neck as he is startled in sudden fear

"What's the matter baby, why won't you look at me?"

He replies, "I can't right now, my eyes burn and cannot see"

He tells this little lie to not face distress and pain

Because engraved in his mind is someone else, another name

As he starts to think deeper, his heart beats faster and faster

In a relationship with a lie, causing pain no joy or laughter

Like the 80/20 rule, 80% will put in the time

Make the mistake of crossing the line, and 20% is all you'll find

Resting on the balcony every night to stare at stars

Shaking his head in misery because his life has fell apart

He looks over his shoulder to see her sleeping in bed

Looks back at the stars and continues to shake his head

Cherish the love you have, it may only come one time

Slip up and throw it away and it will linger in your mind

Now your mind is in the clouds, the clock ticks and fades away

Now you're left with one thought, about…

"The Regrets of Yesterday"

Like Father, Like Son...

In your shoes as a young boy, they were too big, I couldn't fill
I stood tall and tried to walk, but would fall back down the hill
But as I got older, it was my posture to help me stand
And filling up your shoes is what shaped me into a man
I am strong because of you, you gave me light when I couldn't see
You gave me everything I needed, you said be all that you can be
You paved out the road, you left me with a plan
You told me never quit, don't be that "Trapped in Sorrow" man
I love you for who you are, and for everything that you did
Sacrifices were made, ever since I was a kid
The family will mourn, we will cry because you're you
But you're living pain free, with your Mom and Dad too
It just doesn't feel right, to not have you here with me
But I know you're Spirit lives, and it's you I want to be
The Heavens gained an Angel, they will all rejoice and dance
Because your heart was pure gold, you gave everyone a chance
From the Cardinals and the Bees, to the Butterflies and the trees
I know you will send me signs, I know you will be pleased
Now I have a boy, who I raise and looks to me
I know we'll be OK, because you taught me who to be
May your body rest in peace, your work here is done
And nothing can break our bond, because.... Like Father,
Like Son...

Words Coated in Gold

My words define art, art is what I claim

Because of what I claim, my pen has no timeframe

Surrounded by these trees creating paper with all these leaves

A yellow ink found in my pen

With a passion planted like seeds

I just can't stop, even when I seem to think hard

Producing words off my tongue

A brains thought is like stars

I will reach for planet Mars and stream success from planet Earth

Put in the time to make it work and I will show you what it's
   worth

How is art found, in words, verbs, and nouns?

A color with silent sounds, expresses a mind that's quite profound

If my words define art, and my pen has no timeframe

Writing in the future, present, and past; creates realms our
   minds can tame

Living in a world, that's opposite from what we see

A pen creates gold, like the treasures lost at sea

I am a picture-less theme, and this passion will not grow old

Creating "Words on Fire", is also…

"Words Coated in Gold"

The Circle of Life

Have you ever wondered, about your presence here on earth?

A breathless lined up seed linked to Mom's who give you birth

How are we chosen, to represent this life?

Living on a board game, taking chances with our dice

What's the meaning of a life span, why must we die?

Do we return back to earth, with a different pair of eyes?

I've been here before, to remember with no clue

Was it from another life, a glimpse of Déjà vu?

People keep being born, but our time seems to end

Do we end our life in sins, or born to try again?

Years go by, and time seems to fly

Our world looks the same, but it's aging in disguise

An out of body experience, a realm we cannot see

With Heaven above and Hell beneath, so what's in between?

A mysterious satisfaction, to feel pain from cries and laughter

Grasping onto life, being afraid from what will happen

The shape of our world, is it circle? Is it a globe?

It's not a moving probe; it holds stories to be told

So, what would it be like, to die and be born twice?

Is our time-line eternally straight, or is it called "The Circle of
Life"

Failure on Earth

This world was created to bring happiness and peace
Taken over by sin, as these years have increased
How do we stop the pain, and from destroying this place?
Not caring for other lives and disrespecting each race
Mother Nature is mad because the weather is strange
Many people have passed, because of hijacked planes
You want to make a difference in this world full of hate
But it's hard to break the mind of all the devilish snakes
How much more can we take, when our world is fake?
And the Government doesn't care about the lives at stake
The root of all evil could cause a life to be sour
But nobody cares because money is power
The man over there lying on the ground with bugs
Doesn't need food, because he depends on drugs
The girl on the corner trying to make a few bucks
Was wrongfully accused, now her life is screwed up
So, what's your story, will you plant your deed here on Earth?
Or play the victim role and say your life's been cursed
Don't get caught up in lies and frames
Sitting behind bars creates a mind-shift game
Every time I think, that things could be worse
Yes! That's quite true, with all the "Failure on Earth"

Falling Skies

Sometimes we feel pressure, from life and what it brings

Like trapped inside a hive, you're alive, but Bees sting

You sit and shake your head because you feel like it's the end

The ground shakes beneath your feet, and what's' above is
   sinking in

Do you sit and do nothing, while wishing for better times?

Or stand up and move forward, and proceed to free your mind?

Some people can't find the exit, from that hive and all those stings

So, they sit soaked in honey, which holds down their open wings

Don't sit and let life, just rain down on your parade

We all go through struggles, even the flowers in the shade

You're a seed that's been planted, and your blessings is the rain

So, grow in your soil and live that life that you proclaim

Your eyes see dark clouds, but your heart can see bright rays

Swim freely through the world, and don't get guided by the waves

So, remove all that honey that holds you down and start to rise

Or you'll find yourself stuck, looking up at...

"Falling Skies"

A Reunited Thought ~
(Part 3 Final)

Their walking along this path, feeling sad about older days

In the past they walked this path, so Déjà vu stole their gaze

Leaves are falling down, other couples are passing by

The poem "Her Thoughts of Him" was on the ground which
  caught his eye

He stops to take a break, and sits down to embrace her thoughts

He decides he'd like to walk, but drops a note, about his thoughts

Five minutes later, comes a girl who wears a frown

Crying while looking down, "His Thoughts of Her" is what
  she found

Was this meant to be, to have emotions crossing paths?

Or will the two sit in silence and continue the thoughts they have?

While he was smelling laundry, inhaling up her scent

She was writing in her journal about the times they spent

He turns around and starts to run, heading toward her home

It's time to break the ice, living like this, he won't condone

Sprinting really fast to reach his other half

He bumps into a girl holding the note he used to have

Staring in the eyes of tears from girl and guy

A hug for affection, a love they can't deny

These are life's lessons, follow your heart and what you're taught

Now their hearts beat together, creating "A Reunited Thought"

From Rags to Riches

Feeling down and depressed, I'm cold, I'm stressed

I feel awake when I sleep, no warmth, no sheets

No family, no friends…no house to live in

So how do I survive, when all I do is cry?

We all have a purpose, isn't that how life goes?

Searching up and down, for something God only knows

I sleep here, I sleep there, from a sewer to a chair

I want to wash my face, I want to brush my hair

Lord show me the way, please bless me with some food

You said you'd never leave me, your child that cries to you

I came across a man, who gave me paper and a pen

He said I have a calling, and my struggles reached the end

I didn't know what to think, I didn't know what to write

My minds filled with fog, but I'll write about my life

A few months later, I bless kids and their wishes

By telling my life story, and living "From Rags to Riches"

Where Beauty is Found

You are amazing, and I love who you are

It lies in your heart and within the stars

The sound of the breeze as it sways across the sea

The sound of your voice and smile from cheek-to-cheek

Expand your horizons and soar across the sky

It's all around you, just open up your eyes

From a flower to a Beetle, a Bee to a Siegel

A tropical colored fish, to the American Bald Eagle

Even if you're blind and cannot see, just listen closely, to hear
  beauty plays keys

Listen to the melody, let it seep in your ears

The rustling of the leaves, from the running of deer's

Listen to the waves as they splash against the rocks

And now hear your inner voice with imaginable thoughts

So now that you can see and hear ravishing sounds

This is a small list of "Where Beauty is Found"

The New World

This world is considered 4 and a half billion years old

Is it time for the end, and a new story to be told?

Scientists predicts that our world will end

Even if it does, will new life form begin?

So, listen closely and think about what's told

As the beginning of the end will start to take mold

We've always followed Ancestors and Disciples

But somewhere hidden is a buried new cycle

So, everything is gone, except a person and a place

That 'X' marks the spot, another realm of human race

But this world is different, much bigger than before

All planets lined up, like a shopping mall of stores

Four times bigger, perfect weather, no winters

Maybe Heaven is on Earth, right in the core and centered

Everywhere you look, will be mirrors for you to see

To reflect back on this world, where life form used to be

Don't get scared to see life after death

You're now living somewhere else, that's just hidden from the rest

When this world's gone, everything's OK

Because "The New World" begun, to take the old worlds place

Paint Your Perfect Scene

Imagine the possibilities if you could draw how to live

My life's canvas is titled "Help," and I define the word give

So, pull out your brush and create your destiny

Life is your red carpet, so be the artist you want to be

If you have a special passion, you're now a brush stroke away

If you take it off of paper, mold that passion out of clay

When drawing out your life, make sure others can feel and hear

If it's all about yourself, then your portrait will start to smear

You might be feeling down, feeling stuck and want to stray

The hands-on clocks will tick, and those times will fade away

You can't just sit and stare, and say, "Oh I wish…"

If you want to reach the top, positivity must exist

Your picture is almost finished, it may be crooked like a spine

But in order to straighten it out, you must color between the lines

So, fill your life with colors, and portray them as your dream

Follow the path of success, like water flowing down a stream

So now that you're done, hold it up like a screen

And admire this fine art, called "Paint Your Perfect Scene"

My Guardian Angel

I am alive, I live, and I breathe

I am protected from above by a Spirit I cannot see

When I am frightened, she is there

When I am depressed, she is aware

She coats me with her love and covers me with her wings

I am guarded by an Angel, who can do unimaginable things

She was assigned to me from the start, knew me when I was a seed

When I cry for help, her presence is felt, especially when I'm
    in need

My heart is sincere, for my Angel, that's guarding over my life

Thank you Jesus, for my Angel, she's perfect and just right

So, when I go to sleep tonight, I will smile at the air

Because I know I will sleep peacefully with my Guardian Angel
    there....

Message from the Author:

Fun Fact: I wrote this poem when I was in high school. That was about 20 years ago, you can still make your dreams happen. The right moment will be called within divine timing. Never give up!

His Road to Salvation

He was left in the rain, no shoes and clothes stained

Becoming a man at age 5, without love became pain

It's eating at his soul that he was left to be alone

Sleeping on concrete, with no food and sore bones

Looking at the stars as tears drip from his eyes

Reciting a soft prayer to ease his insides

Searching for a family, and a place to call home

Overlooked by the world, a hard life, is like stone

But I see him in my dreams, my heart beats for his pain

The urge to save his life is a calling I shall claim

But he fears me…he's afraid of what I'll do

I told him he's saved now, and his prayer survived too

Reaching out my hand, telling him that I'm here

Not everyone is cruel in this world you have feared

His skin looks weak and his body seems bruised

Using a table as shelter, should be the place to provide food

He stares at me now, just looking up and down

The thinking he portrays, creates a silent sound

I told him it's OK, and that I'm here for a reason

There's four parts in a year, and I'll be here for each season

He smiles and seems happy, no more tears and starvation

This is his new path, called "His Road to Salvation"

I Can Hear your Pain

Shhhhh! Listen closely, something is not right

I hear painful heartbreak wounds, from an emotional lost fight

Did I stumble into something, that I hear what's meant to feel?

To hear cries for help, and express words to help them heal

Maybe I can touch, that pain that's in your heart

And spread comfort under your skin, to give you a fresh start

You have to be strong, in this world full of hate

Because I hear your tears crying, that's running down your face

Don't get caught up, in yourself versus fate

And stomping one's heart, until the life of it breaks

Time heals wounds, so stand strong and hold on

You're the doctor in this picture, so prescribe some move on

If you could hear pain, it's like a prisoner on your side

Just beating on your body and stating the heart died

I want you to know, that I hear your suffering pain

I'll protect you through your storm, and cover you when it rains

Not only that, I'll place my heart against yours

Breathe life in your body, until the pains been destroyed

I'm a special human being, the only one that remains

Not only can I feel, I can ease and "Hear your Pain"

An Unknown Era

It was never recorded, but it existed throughout time
And in this line of time, one life was blessed to find
"Awake from your dream, with brain created scenes!!"
The images are engraved, I found historical human beings
The prehistoric ape replicates the human shape
Here their bones are steel, perfect limbs without breaks
No need to work out, everyone's the same mass
Could it be that "Opposite World," with green skies and
     blue grass?
If this was never found, how did I stumble upon this place?
Creating a mind shift race, gives the word "imagery" some taste
Will I go down in history for this place you can't see?
Or should I create a prototype, in museums it shall be
Flowers you pick and eat, this place is different and quite neat
Technology is discrete, but their brain defines unique
How does the world compete, and are lives don't seem complete?
Does the circle of life exist, or is it buried beneath our feet?
Time after time, raises questions about time
Is day and night real, or has our perception crossed the line?
Our world is known as planet Earth, in ancient times "The Terra"
I'm the founder of this special place, which I call…
"An Unknown Era"

A Child's Birdie

Help!! Mommy...Help!! I'm stuck and can't breathe
But his cries for help hurt, so he's forced to not scream
Everything is silent, from the trees and the Bees
But along came a Birdie, for a boy and his needs
The boy falls asleep, a heart with no beat
Out comes Mom, raining tears on concrete
The Birdie starts to chirp, "You're saved on this day"
And the EMT's arrived to help take the pain away
Several hours later, arrives a Dad who shall see
His son in bed saying, "Daddy come hold me"
The boy feels no pain, perfect heart and brain
Lying in bed praying for the bird that came
Look!! Mommy...Look!! That Birdie saved my life
Others wore green, but the main one was all white
The baby has been saved, the baby's alright
I saw you hold me tight, for my life you did fight
A Mother sheds tears, in happiness with no fears
Thanks to a Spirit...a Birdie who's now here
Could it be true, to have an experience this early?
Or is my son's Guardian Angel, named...
"A Child's Birdie"

I Can, and I Will

Somebody tried to tell me, there are certain things I couldn't do
Like my life has loose screws, and that I'd fail and always lose
But the passion in this man will look past those negative chants
Because dancing with the devil means that evil has no chance
"Well, what do you mean by dance? Stepping in sync to hold
    evil's hands?"
"Wouldn't that make you follow the wrong blueprint and
    awful rants?"
No, I am happy, and I dance when I am free
So, dancing with the devil means he cannot get through to me
I'm a poetic color, I'm a vision on the rise
I'm the ink on this paper, and this passion never dies
See people will break you down, they will laugh in your face
That's because they're jealous, of all the success you've embraced
Life is a race, and our stepping stones have different tastes
So always wear a smile, and you will always solve your case
Those people who say you can't, they'll call you names like a bum
But once you get it done, now they're the ones that's looking
    dumb
So, stamp your name in the world, negative vibes will always kill
Don't ever say you can't, just say,
"I Can, and I Will…"

The Angel by Your Side

The Lord said you're blessed and that you're favored on this land

If you want to understand, pay attention to what's at hand

Be thankful for your life, and running this path that's a race

Because the figure by your side has held your hand amongst
   this place

Think about those times you were mad for running late

A car crash was on your route, so running late, was not a mistake

What about that voice that says do this instead of that?

That figure by your side is that voice that has your back

We sit and try to think, to understand we've been warned

Pondering back and forth, a mind clouded by inner storms

But that figure is always there, in the times when things are
   wrong

Your broken and feeling weak, so for you that figure is strong

A mirror shows reflection, and our shadows by our side

If our shadow is always there, is it that figure that I describe?

How could you show hate, towards the ones who made mistakes?

Mistakes creates a path, a new road for us to take

You are shielded in every way, you've been comforted when
   you've cried
You get stronger every day because of
"The Angel by Your Side…"

A Loving World

You can touch a heart today, with a smile on your face

This world full of hate, should be destroyed and replaced

Give a helping hand, to the man with no home

And don't stare at the woman, that's bruised with broken bones

That child over there, whose heart is going to crash

Just say a simple prayer, "With strength your pain won't last"

That's the type of confidence, and prayers that exist

When we tend to need help, we're mind painting out a wish

We all may be different, but our hearts the same kind

So to say, "Love is blind" should not apply to this time

Open up your soul, and touch the lives around the earth

Show off love like a Mother, like after giving birth

We often show our pain, that's been buried like remains

A stranger needs your help, but you ignore and refrain

Be protective of your enemies, and pray their souls be saved

The temple of God is in you, a new road will now be paved

Now that you can see, a heart that's pretty as pearls

How would you like to live, in what's now…

"A Loving World"

Her Dark Twisted Paradise

She awakes, but her mind is still sleep

The screaming in the streets, brings terror to her sheets

Stepping out her home, to a world that's so hot

The sun falling on the lands, of an Earth which now's rot

She's nervous, she screams, "My baby boy please!"

This world seems over, like the burning of the trees

To the skies turning black and the grounds split in twos

She was determined to find her son, she was determined to
  not lose

Her mind jumps while she rests, her family now she could
  not find

Strangers crossed her path, saying come and join our line

She couldn't, she panicked, her son she could not find

This platform we must board, because this is the end of time

A weight on her shoulders, and her stomach starts to sink

She was pulled on this platform before she could even think

Tears filled her eyes, and sorrow took her soul

A stranger says I'm sorry, that this world was so cold

High up in the sky, the heat of disaster can still be felt

But inside this woman mourns, her life feels crushed, her heart
   just melts
But there's more to what's next, do you know where you will go
Climb inside this portal because you're now in the know
The door opens to show her fate, and she sees to her surprise
A beautiful golden kingdom, white doves and bright skies
Stepping out to explore, this new land she seeks to find
That weight just disappeared, her heart says her son is fine
From the Diamond coated waters and the grapes to praise
   your life
She awakes from her dream...   "A Dark Twisted Paradise

You are More

When you look in the mirror, please do tell, what do you see?

Are you reflecting your true self, or hiding what you can be?

Do you really think this life is the limit to who you are?

Your mind may be planted here, but your dreams can carry far

Society and its rage, you will see it your whole life

The emotion, the pain, is like a stabbing from a knife

But you have what it takes, to heal your every bruise

You will make it in this realm, you will win, and not lose

They will try to suppress your mind, they will try to keep you
down

The secrets of life are around you, but your vision has not
been found

It's time to wake up, do you see who you are?

You can create your own reality, you're the driver, and life's
your car

So, expand your conscious mind, and realize what lies before

You are living the human experience, so please believe that "You
are More"

Spending the Day with Jesus

What a historical day, I spent it with Jesus

Giving the hungry some food and blessing children with
    sneakers

Traveling the world, with a snap of my fingers

To heal broken hearts that got shattered to pieces

It's so amazing to have power and be loved

Handing new Angels their wings like doves

We walked across the ocean, how incredibly fun

Controlling Winter, Spring, Fall and the hot Summer sun

I was taught how to cure, the people that can't see

Answering prayers as they smiled and praised me

Jesus looked at me and said close your eyes

And open them up to find a pleasant surprise

As my vision got dark and my heart beat harder

I opened my eyes quickly to find my Grandfather

As I start to shed a tear, he caught them with his wings

Saying don't cry you're favored to do remarkable things

Then I thought to myself, well what does he mean?

He said you've been chosen as that special human being

I quickly looked at Jesus as He softly touched my head

My eyes suddenly closed and my imagination spread

I heard soft voices say today you have pleased us

And a special human being got to spend it with Jesus.

The Love of a Mother

It's amazing how we got here

We came from our Mom

A very special woman, who taught right from wrong

To be our guiding light, and show us the right way

To shield us with her heart, and teach us how to pray

A Mother's heart is pure, and bigger than Earth

And that heart grows bigger, on the day that she gives birth

Reflect on those days, when your Mother stated "No!"

Don't get mad and disrespect, what's best a Mother knows

You're the cub of a Queen, who can do all things

Mind and body strong, a super natural light being

Moms know all, and they protect throughout the storm

Seeing through fake emotions, to see a heart's been torn

If Moms didn't exist, there would be dark blue skies

Thank you Lord for Moms, they're some Angels in disguise

Love and cherish Moms, because the day they go away

Our hearts will fill empty and our days will now be grey

Our Moms are very special, take the time to love and hug her

And nothing will compare, to "The Love of a Mother"

The Day I Touched the Clouds

Colors turn color, I can't describe what I see

I can't describe what I feel, because my minds lost at sea

Is it because I'm high off life, and my vision never fades?

Or does my smile wake you up, like the breeze from ocean waves?

Never will I stop, and think twice about a dream

On those nights I dream, I create reality from visual scenes

Drenched from the rain, a shiver passes from the snow

My words provide light, and they shine like Heavens glow

As I smile upon this man, he drips tears into his hand

Shaking at his knees makes it hard for him to stand

Sitting on his throne looking down on top of Earth

The Lord points me out, saying "You're blessed so make it work"

I smile once again, and say, "Excuse me sir"

Today the pain will end, and good things will now occur

The man is shaken up, and going down like a sunken boat

I told him the Universe called, for me to deliver this prosperous
    note

Providing peace across the land and touching souls amongst
    these crowds

Now I can tell my story about "The Day I Touched the Clouds"

The Most Fascinating, Person I Never Met

Who are you? Because I have seen you many times

And in my line of time, what I see, I cannot find

For a while you were a blur, like the vision from alcohol

Stumble down, pass out and fall, now you're asleep like
darkness falls

I have tried to reach out, I have tried to lend a hand

But addiction has consumed, this man who cannot stand

There's no love, but so much pain, can you see the tears and
frowns

Your organs are the passengers, your body's plane is crashing
down

But I have Faith in this man, he is someone I never knew

My mind says to hate, but my heart says stay true

Accepting what he is, has caused his life to be a race

To finally face the music and all those lies he embraced

When his face meets his palms, and those tears run down his hand

He looks to the clouds, saying, "I'm sorry, please help me stand"

He has touched all the hearts that has been broken by his rage

At the center of a stage, preaching to the misbehaved

He talks about his pain, and now saves many lives

His smile is now bright, like a sun that's on the rise

He has touched many souls living a life without regrets

And this is "The Most Fascinating, Person I Never Met"

Life After Death

Your vision starts to fade, it's getting dark, your feeling free

And all you feel is love, in this place you now can see

Your body starts to tingle, because you are covered with
Angel spray

Your whole life has been cleansed, and yours sins have
washed away

You float up to the gates, which are surrounded by all white
clouds

A glowing figure holds a book, who looks at you and says,
"I'm proud"

"Welcome back my child, it's so good to have you home"

You have raised your consciousness and this paradise is now
your throne

So, come and follow me, it's time to get your hovering ring

After that please bow down, so I can attach your golden wings

These colors that you see, they don't exist on planet Earth

The last time they crossed your path, was on the day your
Mother gave birth

See, it lies within the Spirit, and not reality

We all have the power, and your mindset is the key

This is life after the physical, it's perfection to the T

Drinking wine and eating grapes, you are awake and now
can see

So welcome home my child, soak it in and take a breath

Because this is paradise, this is now "Life After Death"

The Awakening

Something was suddenly different, and like a switch, my mind
    had just changed

And not the type of the change where you sit and decide
    between two things

There's that feeling of being stuck, now I'm here and can't go back

Shape shifting in a vortex, seeing lost knowledge society lacks

I'm always in my head, questioning this and wondering that

But how did I get here, who woke me up, from that long nap

It's like layers over my eyes have been peeled away to reveal

The true meaning to life, a direction human race, has barely
    steered

Trust the process see, you will walk deep within the fog

Searching within that midst, for the answers to it all

Your mind is like a sponge, you will crave more and try to find

And to always expand the mind, is increasing consciousness
    over time

But why do I feel so lost, shaking my head like my soul's been
    blind?

Trapped inside our human, those answers we scream for, are
    hard to find

But I know that I am more, and what's hidden, is surely bright

Our battle is not the physical, but the Realm of Darkness and
Spiritual light

I woke up... I feel free, but disconnected at the same time

The best way to describe it, is to write these words that lingers
my mind

That feeling of separation, solitude will creep real fast

I must remain in my Spirit, recycled patterns have finally passed

You're evolving, and it's strange, because you never felt this way

Your entire world has been shaken, like a tornado on your best day

Grow into you, and fine tune your true self

Raise your vibration and put old ways up on a high shelf

You are not alone, on this path you seek to find

An "Awakening" is now active, as your soul cries out to the
Great Divine...

Poetry is Me

It seems all I need is this pen and pad see

Because my mind flows like wind, overtop of the world's seas

As these thoughts cross my path and my brain starts to race

My words are like skittles, a colored rainbow you might taste

I will take you on a journey, my pen creates many sightings

I am engraved on the paper and defined by my writings

I will write anything, and never be limit to one thing

From nature, love and sorry – to an Angel with strong wings

The portraits in my head, are pictures drawn over time

Transfer it to paper and see this writer's mind

I live, I write

I cry, I fight

I'm strong, I'm weak

I'm a color, unique

I'm here, I'm there

I'm a brush to paint scenes

If you want to make a difference, be my guest, by all means

I'm going to touch this world, reaching out with a large grasp

And over time I will prevail, so I flipped my hour glass

So, with my pen and my pad is all I need and you'll see

Because this life that I live means, "Poetry is Me"

Conclusion

Thank you for purchasing and taking the time to read *"Poetry is Me"* written by Kevin E. Brown. This is the first book published by this author, but it's certainly not his last. *"Poetry is Me"* is breathtaking, and hopefully it left you in awe while visualizing each poem that gets painted to the forefront of your mind. No matter what trials and tribulations you might be experiencing, there is a poem in this book that is written just for you.

It had always been a dream of Kevin's to publish his collection of work in a well thought out visual masterpiece. After losing his Father in 2018, his thoughts and emotions never seemed to end. However, between his awakening and his passion for writing, it kept him up late at night creating and redirecting his focus onto paper. *"Poetry is Me"* was written to help you grow, to help you see, to help you understand, to help you think, and simply for your pure love of reading poetry.

If you would like to follow this author for more of his work or to learn more about Spirituality, Personal Growth & Development, or in need of some Life Coaching; you can search and contact Kevin on the following social media platforms below:

Instagram: @Expressed_Wordz
Twitter: @Expressed_Wordz
Facebook: @ExpressedWordz
YouTube: ExpressedWordz

May all of your dreams come to pass because the VICTORY is already yours. Now, it's time to claim it!